PRAISE FOR *A PLEA FOR SECULAR GODS*

"Though not a practicing Catholic, Bryan D. Price's *A plea for secular gods* is imbued with prayerful strangeness and surreal piety. In these irreverently reverent poems, Price captures what it means to be a work in progress, yearning toward faith. In 'The Bystander,' the beleaguered speaker intones 'these are the last / days there are no more oceans to speak of no means / of full immersion in the baptismal font'; his yearning to be reconfigured, if not reborn, is palpable. Both quasi-religious and elegiac, Price takes us to places where 'debris flows fill the house with frogs … where we go to take pictures of other people's pain,' yet the hope of being saved is never far off, as in 'who couldn't use a makeshift altar / a place to just be.' I admire this book for its candor and exactitude, for reminding me of the importance of questing toward something to put our faith in, even if we keep coming smack up against 'a little silhouette of misunderstanding,' even if 'memories … fall off like fingernails or a crow's bill or else throw themselves into the ocean.'" —MARTHA SILANO

WHAT BOOKS PRESS

AN IMPRINT OF

THE GLASS TABLE

COLLECTIVE

LOS ANGELES

A PLEA FOR SECULAR GODS: ELEGIES

A PLEA FOR SECULAR GODS: ELEGIES

BRYAN D. PRICE

WHAT
BOOKS
PRESS

LOS ANGELES

Library of Congress Cataloging-in-Publication Data

Names: Price, Bryan D., 1976- author.
Title: A plea for secular gods : elegies Bryan D. Price.
Description: Los Angeles : What Books Press, 2023. | Summary: "Poems about
    families who do not talk anymore and strange manhoods shared across
    generations, about memories of catastrophic failures, and the
    disappointment that entails being human"-- Provided by publisher.
Identifiers: LCCN 2023024885 | ISBN 9798986625812 (paperback)
Subjects: LCGFT: Poetry.
Classification: LCC PS3616.R5246 P57 2023 | DDC 811/.6--dc23/eng/20230714
LC record available at https://lccn.loc.gov/2023024885

Cover art: Gronk, *Untitled*, mixed media on paper, 2022
Book design by ash good, www.ashgood.com

What Books Press
363 South Topanga Canyon Boulevard
Topanga, CA 90290

WHATBOOKSPRESS.COM

For my father and my mother and their parents.
All of whom haunt these poems.
And, as always, for Claire.

CONTENTS

Peu de gens devineront combien il a fallu être triste
pour entreprendre ressusciter Carthage.

[Few will suspect how sad one had to be to undertake
the resuscitation of Carthage.]

—-Gustave Flaubert (via Walter Benjamin.
From the latter's "On the Concept of History")

MOTTO

my father died like this in
the desert regional medical
center—shriveled up like the
fallen jacaranda flowers

that bees die sucking on
someone wrote in the
guestbook: this is a plea for
secular gods not horses…

THE BYSTANDER

THEOGONY

first there was the god
of last stands
doubling as the spirit
of the waxing year
the patron saint of revolutions
(both just and unjust)
took the knife that originally severed
heaven from earth
covered it in lambskin like
a hand covering a fist and
buried it between
sheets of plain white paper
between onionskin
after the suicide of
a former lover there came
a screed of little acts
mostly profane and necessarily
somber some with
morphine and once
with cyanide
left a note that read—
in the ruins of the internet
there are tapes of me
we can listen to them together
I'm in the honeycomb
in the hive with you

ORALITY

traveling with you sans zygote to Moraga or Orinda

where you live and the hills are like stars on the lens

painted so intuitively into a memory that it narrates itself

eclipses all other genres of remembrance: myths memorials

tall tales origin stories immigrant songs exile orality

ANTELOPE

was that an atomic disaster or just
the sun reflecting off the windows of a train
I am on the toilet reading about obscure saints
I thought you'd be coming in the dead
of night like a fractal or ghost
but there's quite a few moments of daylight left
she asked why are you taking that lighter into
the garage with you that's how marriages end
and I put something pastoral on something
with feathers instead of a skin I learned to play
the guitar sometime between Bush stealing
the election and 9/11 around the time I was
writing the abortion story I have everything in
milk crates from then it's all in pink ink (the
cheapest I could find) someone needs to
write the history of nostalgia from stranded
soldiers to the end of men and then sketch the
moon and its oceans for me or maybe just its
phases from dark navy to the most pathologically
intense neon (or the other way around) no
one knows why I'm like this once the men in
my family put a gun into my ear like I was
the antelope hung my body over the Colorado
river its vein of blood red sand opening
bright like the creation of continuous time

THE BYSTANDER

walking into the kind of twilight where the sun is
still exacting in spots I watch a person prone to
drink overdo it and spill themselves as if through
a funnel the sharp smell of wine-red vomit (familiar to
those of us who have spent a lifetime among alcoholics
sneaking across decay) sours the air indefinitely all
of the old uncles had problems with emphysema four
gone now it was either that or cancer—throat lungs
bladder &c. without stomachs no one could eat anymore
yet we would still go out to the same wooded cemetery
to hunt after unlikely deer careful amongst natives
still pasturing their own sheep these are the last
days there are no more oceans to speak of no means
of full immersion in the baptismal font that code of
being was unconsciously dictated like genetics or more
likely communicated through mimicry problems with
kidneys and livers exacerbated by fine blood and querulous
rages the funerary aspect of such a temperament hangs
heavy over all affairs the apartment as dry and airy
now as desert land stretching out into a matrilineal
gravesite archipelago in the shape of a new moon

ELEGY WITH THANK-OFFERING

out of the thin pink light of an early June morning
it smelled like Albuquerque—like a last bath of
rain on a deep-veined boulevard or a thousand orange
horses like peach trees rotting in the immaculate sun
like a light film of cigarette ash on gun oil
or a collection of bones (the place where Jesus wept)
like the dirt under a palm reader's fingernails or Lourdes
right after the war like a blue field of leeks gone to
seed or a bowl of fresh cut flowers for eating
like a thatched hat used to collect our losses
or the crud that gathers on the walls of a sanitarium or jail
like a basin of holy water used to perfume the skin
or Trinity about an hour before sunrise (the reaper's
reaper) like Diazepam and honeybees like sirens loathe to
sing and the fresh orange leaves left as a thank-offering
for the safe ferrying of a suicidal aunt

SWIMMING IN A RIVER, 1956

I may as well stop writing after this
after going online to hear its call

I thought of my mother's song
and then my aunt's not as beautiful

but like three swimmers swimming
or intricately contrapuntal music

their mother not running because
where is there to sing to—

just languishing in the water like
a utopian idea that ends in decay

TO DISTINGUISH BETWEEN EVERYTHING AND ALMOST EVERYTHING

I meant to meditate on Saturday
now the time is out of joint always
worried fragile anxious—naked
as if coming out of the shower
the next day going into cornfields
the smell and color of a jackdaw's nest
where all and none are welcome
among the poison in the streams
among the whole line of catacombs
from the age of permanent revolution
from the age of Athene when
fatherhood was not recognized—
conception being attributed to the wind

YOU WON'T BELIEVE THIS

you won't believe this
but I am reading Hamlet again—
an old copy with uncut pages
and the death-mask frontispiece
I am not taking it seriously but
it's been open by my side
quiet enough to hear someone
fussing with a pot and its lid
a man showering a footstep on
old wood that's lost its click
something doesn't sit right this
nuclear midnight—preferring
ugly music subtle yet discordant
to the point of certain death
like the dialectical imagination
that severs dreams by dragging
a nail across the curtain—
very quietly like a birdcall

MAGNIFYING GLASS

at some appointed time I'll open the windows
let the sun and pagan air in and like Tantalus I'll stare
into a mirror while I tie a string around the torso
to subdue the nightingale instinct

it is your turn to transgress mine to interpose or accept
yours to devour mine to be eaten
at some appointed time I'll let more than just air in
sky will be empty as a gulag and it will be time for the

kind of Sisyphean tasks with no head-body connections—
three crucifixions or a stuck dream about our S&M glory
very few decisions almost no intentionality
very tiny—the content of our fantasies but the form is

quietist and then political (as in degraded)
the amoralist among us says the earth is the moon
and vice versa one looks green-blue the other the bluest
blue-green in the end it is the eye that seduces

TRANSGRESSION/REPENTANCE

this is not about cognitive decline or
our life together held in place with safety pins
I am driving again and reading Robert Graves
found a volume of his myths in a Santa Maria bookstore
the pages dead leaf yellow and as cold as the day
before the paroxysm—you sprayed me down
black out drunk on the fire escape my psyche
held together between your thumb and blue forefinger
and now thought of as an astral projection or
a separate piece of history: a person who could have been
a sea captain or sister to the son of his old age

DIALOGUES OF THE DEAD

take me on a leash to see the figure of Orion
take me to the border between wash and disembowel
take me on a rope to forgive the rope
take the rope and make it into a damnable end
a preamble to waking
to making a fetish of
like turnable handles
and gentle latches for escaping
walk me leave me omit me
release me from natural history
obscure me with a scrim
with muslin with an aporia
withstand me withdraw from me
do not alienate abolish me

LATE OCTOBER

Night spreads her greenness
wet as a raincoat

across your shoulders
double-sexed and winged

like Eros green
as the sweetest acorn

oceanic green
textured with bluish hairs

a green now lost out of
memory

cell by cell
marked out of time

like waning symbols
of emphatic

difference
only ether remains

as green as Night
rising naked from Chaos

HORSEMANSHIP

saw a Susan Rothenberg painting and thought
about how I wanted to disappear into that
universe knowing nothing about horsemanship
I just found it heretical and I wanted to be inside
some timeless expression of doubt take the human
essence out of the center of everything and we
are left with a very different kernel of violence
I doubt I can go on like this for too much longer
but one day I'd like to see myself on a cave wall
running after or being chased by a beast or a
deer—a metaphor for your death cult and mine

INSOMNIA

NONLINEAR MEMOIR

late in the day maybe early pink sky in bed cultivating transmissions with watery

gray looking through the book of words and phrases in the bath with the Cyclops

trying to draw out the primal scream paintbrush gripped between my knees just in

case there are no mirrors—I wouldn't expect you to understand or be understood

the task of the biographer is to differentiate between mountains and sea this is from

a vision or recollection I have of Anna wearing a green hospital shirt—a dream and

not a dream or covenant between being and wanting to forgive the snow for falling

NATURE WRITER

or life after wolf
went out to the woods with
pecans and an egg
to ascertain or write about

a certain species of death—
death by animal melancholia
painfully self-aware
of skin over fur

body greeted softly by
an ocean of light and then
overtaken by flame
floor gently patterned

with muck dried by
the rays of the sun into
fuel—energy for the last
stand and final judgment

when history casts
away old names like disused
lungs and sprouts wings
instead of a memory

YEAR 29

such things have been worn away
tried and true things like shoes
skin and posture it is the posthuman
rain even buildings crease
and fold—quiver in the wind
the acceleration of age on the faces
of the apple trees can be detected
by the tv eye nothing granted
by either gods or moons except
for sleep where even dreams have
become grainy from the laughter
of decay there is no alcohol
left to rub on the skin grafts only
petroglyphs prefiguring the aesthetic
of lists—indices of pure derangement
rules laws threats from above
along the lines of we have come
for your children and your
children's horses and every other
fragment of bone not nailed down
such is the logic of late history

KNOCK AT THE DOOR

affirmation or otherwise on the other side with a voice like Lee Ranaldo's
coming through the beaded curtain not too far different from Didion's uncanny
encounter with the world outside or the replicants come to take their revenge
on our control of nature debris flows fill the house with frogs nothing but a dry
lakebed left where we go to take pictures of other people's pain called something
like boy with cigarette or boy with hand grenade or boy coddling eight bird eggs

POEM

poem buried inside a poem buried inside a poem about poems but
really it's a picture of a running horse or a clump of grass not clump
but bush maybe barrel I cannot even look at it curled up in its sheets like
that to see is not to see but to know empirically the way that grotesque
hand curdles shakes trembles us unto dying like the sun plunging into
unspeakable murk this is me crumpled never running like water this is the
last bit of it carried away on a maggoty tide of un-life its inner ear on fire

EXPERIMENTAL NOVEL

maybe about dystopia puzzles mazes labyrinths how
do stories end behavior learned internalized like
breath restored to its former place among the senses
eyes glassy having just pissed in a wine bottle dystopia
is a literature of fleeing—walking scaling crossing
sailing with one's clothes hardened by the saline wind
naked across the channel or breach carrying seeds like
memento mori I keep hidden away separate from and
not subject to the whims of genetically engineered
grasses air is now the color of water and you have
sprouted luminous slimy gills or you are a clone—I am
a clone of you that is how things work in the afterlife
gender neutral or nonspecific wearing comfortable
clothes each thing a different shade of cyan one only
noumenally different from the next it is like Lascaux but
we paint with horsehair and are lazy half-working slightly
dazed machines we are like certain trees or even-toed
ungulates existing according to our elective affinities

TO RENDER PAIN IN ANIMALS

use small words as bitten down as seeds
look deep into the eye past the
sockets past the realm of the immutable
it's like vocalizing the sound of cicadas
waited for you near a fence in western PA
a deer came out of the cemetery and then
another and another the humming was like
the dead sound before a lightning storm
bathe ritualistically (only once or twice)
court suffering and death ask to be
sacrificed the wound is peace to open the
border is to open the skin the rotted peach
had becalmed my spirit do not waste the
command to go forth and reciprocate
the peach was unripe and the floors were just
old boards I took the staples out like any
other superfluity slept in strange positions
gave into breathing (not meditating) just
gesturing toward life and persisting—get
out your watercolor paper and draw a straight
edge do it over and over again in pen in pencil
in scissor and vulture feather keep doing
so until you have made sense of the brutality

I HAVE BEEN REREADING BOOKS

disappearing into deep crags of history all conjured out of

language—resurrected maybe (as it is with certain kinds of taxidermy)

this is the downslope or glottal stop between eras or epochs fatigued

from the heavy lift every last scrap and remnant of your dreambook taken

to a landfill hidden beneath the gentle sound of a crow's feet on leaves—

as scientifically perfect as music

NOVEL AGAINST REALISM

you are writing a disturbing novel against realism in that I cannot
match you word for word you tell me that I am the stranger in your
novel the object of abuse you put to death at the end of this you write:
he was not oblivious to the stares of other people and so he was
tortured stabbed flayed beheaded quartered piled up like rocks with no
dirt thrown on top as it was with Polyneices and desires are everywhere—
rivers silted up with them from years of neglect and everything is the
color of coral (or artichoke): eyes skin walls sky valleys oceans voids
there is an editor's note at the end about Geertz's essay on cockfighting
in Bali this is not a metaphor it says this is not a fable or a *roman à clef*
or autofiction this is make-believe right down to the descriptions of
Charenton you tell me this novel is unspeakably heavy its words as heavy
as the points making up the Star of David in fact they are not words
at all but signals or calls meant to drag the bell of heaven down to
earth and the rock of earth down to hell this is you say not like the shit
you (meaning me) write this is the work of a mighty river crossing
Olympus an oath against realism a war against nature—it is titled *On Love*

INSOMNIA

she says she can produce just the thorax this was not in
a dream but after I got up to feed the cat use the
restroom drink water from the tap I laid back down and
closed my eyes her face was pantomiming childbirth like it
was turning in on itself I immediately go to write down the
word *thorax* force myself to sleep so that I don't look up the
word thorax or think about the next words that may come
out of her mouth she has four or five faces at once I
have insomnia and I once told my wife it is when I see faces
that I know I am going to fall asleep and now I see
anguished eyes and cheeks clotted with tears a face that is
as ordered as speech as legible as decay like the imagination
of coherence she says I can produce a thorax but just the
thorax not the winged feet or Achilles tendon

NO EMPATH

ice cube tray wilts in the sink like everything
else dog eats bird I should shower but I believe
I will shower at midnight when the moon is
cold something grates pricks at the conscience
or soul—the preservation of a continuing assent
a trying to be your animal a kind of mystical
inwardness carried on droplets—on found sounds
excavated from AM radio (late night) eerie
furniture music aural visions of a future with no
ability to fathom sleep as it was intended no
sacred cycle of rebirth and decay days are now
valleys and only beyond the aubade line do we display
our grief—perform it like the art of memory

TROPIC AND DERANGEMENT

as everyone knows books are animals read or unread his voice was very soft

he had been comforted by such voices and there was a thinness to his touch

very light like an insect walking across his arm he reads very inconsistently or

discontinuously reading is a kind of curse (as is desire) he remembered a painting:

black ink on cream-colored cardstock and very faintly between the brushstrokes

there was writing (what some might call text) words or codes that he could

not read either because they were so softly applied to the cardstock or

because he had lost the ability to interpret such things he suggested a backstory

and told him he had fled or was fleeing—an exile alienated by his moorings

and the voices and language of strangers the painting he told him was of a

river that he was navigating he kept turning the pages looking for images in the

sequence or order of words and then in single words detached from reality

machines unto themselves—aesthetic or simple machines that could carry a

story all on their own: *tropic* and *derangement nutmeg meridian perspiration sun-bleached*

sublate nothing symbolic symbols he said were for ideology or worse—politics

and politics was a bloodstain on nature like the old testament or film-noir

nature wasn't pure he said but it had perfect comic timing

PHOTOGRAPHING DISASTERS

I am ready to speak begin first with the length
we can have less something small like an
epilogue appended to the end about what it
meant to absorb so many televangelists in the
seventies (depending on your patience for
digressions) I guess there is nothing that cannot
hurt us the prayer goes up with the plane not
secular or addressed to something as thinly-
veiled as *the universe*—God grant me time very
simple like a line drawing of wrists just like that
I fell asleep holding a rosary purpled with
blood Pearblossom Highway was littered
with fish when the wind took his ashes into
the ruins we were having a very frank
conversation in the shadow of the water-tank
and went inside its belly to hear our voices
strung up together and echoing out of the rot…
then jumped barefoot like birds from the womb

THE POCKET STOICS

it brings an overwhelming sense of sorrow not tears but physical
pain I thought about what it would be like to hear a voice from the
dead giving a yoga or guitar lesson on youtube like background
noise from another room in a stranger's house the two of you asleep
together on the couch something akin to gmail mystically flagging a
seven-year old email from my father that says to me in a knifelike
cadence: yes, room 135 and sometimes it gives me a feeling of solace
like the holy ghost pressing my nose and mouth beneath the surface
of the amniotic bath it may be a synecdoche or representation at the
very least a part or name that stands without resolve for the whole
I don't know if you can hear me but I am happy to have visited the
world's second oldest tree dung-covered and alone liquefied by a stiff
rain I packed an ounce of it into a tin made a paste or paint caked it
onto my hands and face forced some into a glass pipe and smoked
it down to the dregs darkened the interiors and kept darkening until
the page was wet with blood dug in the barrows to desecrate the
survivors consider this an epistolary vision about whether or not the
algorithm intentionally cycles ghosts across the lives of the living—
trafficking us in advice from the tomb

GHOSTS

ALREADY SEEN

I have been thinking of writing something
puzzling over a bizarre theme or set of
themes put down maybe into a story about
suicide I wrote around 2001 or 2 *returning to*
I guess is the right way to say it I thought
I heard you come into the house but it must
have been the apparition of a noise something
unsettling like a premonition am I slipping
off into a bad place the past dispersed into
atoms with no chance of miraculous return
or resurrection seeing from miles away on
the clearest of clear days the bodies of wild
swimmers who are us left adrift but comforted
by warm water (an act of desperation one
summer in Lake Sonoma or somewhere
off the coast of Hawaii) I closed my eyes
and saw my father come out of the bathroom
as I am apt to do sometimes with my belt
undone walking sloppily and then standing
in front of the television with hands on hips
it all began to make sense—this is about
pure subjectivity or the arc of living as a
single curve of unremitting grief punctured
by the smallest recurrences seen from a
mirror or maybe in a movie within a movie

READING SUSAN SONTAG'S DIARIES

I turn to my birthday
or the day closest to my birthday

(August 15, 1976)
she writes—

what does it mean for time to go faster
for it to pass more slowly

Brodsky says there are two subjects:
time and language

I see on page 128 the word [*Bataille*]
in brackets remember

a warm day lying
ignorant and naked on water or

on air or on a bed rapt
listening

to Rebecca tell me the story of the eye...
this moment in time is my

hand-embroidered
found photograph

CORSET

the color of ice or the foamy cap that tops a wave
the color of blindness in a well-lit room
a void that I am next to or is close at hand
something to be dwelled within

exquisite gravitational pull
successful or nearly perfect occlusion
speaks or tells (furtively) over the murmur of cars
and the occasional airplane overhead

rises over the din like a photograph cropped to reveal
something purer than itself as it is with eating the
deer's heart or liver raw an eight minute pause or
interval without dreams or thoughts

as quiet as negative space or the absence of light
the blankness is clear in that it is present
speaking to me in a voice that is adjacent to words
not a howl but like a fracture in the history of speech

SUNDAY MORNING

you sleep in that filthy shirt and then we go to get beer in it
drink it on the street out in the air like lovers do
here the rhythms are the same: do surgery on a dog or a pant leg
wipe one hand over the other avoid the abattoir fate of squirrels
sky looks the same—thunder clouds pink at the edges
even your shoulder blades under the falling ashes
gravity is a machine that devours time but the eye still transcribes
what moves through its field of vision though the photograph
is indecipherable now: a body of water maybe or a painting of where
water once was when about eight thousand violet swallows descended
like fortune tellers imitating the light

GHOSTS

the guitarist Robbie Basho died on a chiropractor's table I
once cut the flowers from a lavender bush and they never
grew back I'd rather you not sing my name but if you choose
to—do so in the style of an avian field recording Shannon
came to the door and asked about Bill—I explained that he
died in the desert not far from here I told her that he may
be watching over us now my mother gave me a crystal to
wear around my neck and claims it is in dreams that the dead
make themselves useful I have a guitar that sits in the attic
and at night it plays itself I have been reading from a book
about birds from a book about trees and shrubs from a book
about French cooking I have gone to the healing waters
that can be seen but not touched I don't want to die by
anyone else's hand I will stay awake until the wind ceases the
rain ceases all chatter erupts into an uncanny valley of silence

THE ÉTUDES

walking through a blue field and then sand and then sun

this I think is where I might lay down to die as a dog does

with heavy grieving teats listening to birds improvise

études repeating and repeating their disembodied

rhymes as legible as Orion's Belt on an acid clear night

like some tiny vaporous correspondence with a

metronome or some other form of artificial intelligence

FROGS

I remember you vividly as day was leaving
the sky grown filthy with clouds

leaves birds witches into cats dogs hares etc.
memory is not obsessive verisimilitude is not

real if they say they have swallowed frogs
believe them it may be a euphemism for death

DIVERS BELL

before the thunder and lightning there
was the terror—

a deep one from the bottoms of time
and then you called on the phone

standing in the kitchen I knew
the kicking sound from before

the diver's bell was conceived
from before even speech was brought

forth to connect all the other elements
standing in the kitchen I knew to

gather up your things and to prepare
myself for very precise dreams of a

second skin that I would come to know
as well my own

POEM FOR M. ROTHKO

I don't know shit about the bowery or growing lavender
I don't know about going cold turkey or tying a noose
I don't know how to paint a house or operate a lathe
I don't know how to fix a guitar or tune a piano
I don't know how to clean load or fire a gun
I don't know how to talk about Mark Rothko or what it means
to wrap a body in plain black muslin in order to set it on fire

PARASAILING

in Puebla we watched
drugged tigers being driven
endlessly around the Zócalo
Haitian guitar music kept us going
I kept a journal on graph paper
that tells me the Beijing Olympics
were on in the hotel bar
after you fell asleep I drank
beer with ice and thought about
the medical instrument museum
there was no parasailing like
in the Denis Johnson
story about stealing copper wire
in my father's house (where
I lived for many years)
he had hung a picture of
himself in the hallway high
above the Gulf of California—
what a lonely business I would
think to myself as lonely as
fighting forest fires or when
the sun hides behind the past
to withdraw its light forever

SELF-LOATHING IS THE POINT

that is what I would have told him if we spoke (or were still speaking)

I don't ask why but I know it to be true despite the need for doctors

and mystics despite the need for the power of positive thinking what

voice is that are you speaking in tongues or doing a bit or superimposing

a truer self or soul I am reminded here of epistemology—of trying to

be your beautiful actor your genuflecting pig blindfolded and staked to the

earth your self-contained vessel of putrid annoyance it has been twelve

minutes since I have thought about the future if I had a son I would

tell him that no matter what has been uttered by other witches or prelates

the self-loathing was the point

ALL MY FRIENDS

measuring myself against photographs of
people who look brushed against the grain of
their own travails like they know how to play
the piano not so much intuitively but with an
ear for watery sounds like car horns in the rain
or the natural reverb of public restrooms and
then later after it gets dark we play one together
on a tarp laid out beneath us really a chord
organ she taught me to play like an ape to repeat
scraps of choruses to scrape together and
get by on nothing in a systematic way that involves
discipline only what the body wants at a certain
point the laughter is suspended to set the whole
machine on fire lay down and self-immolate…

PRESENCE

I dreamt you came out of the ocean led

on a rope or belt—tied it like Cain to a door

and then I heard a sound like the crow makes landing

on a fence with a heavier presence than expected

woke up but kept my eyes closed the way

a soothsayer does when she paints mountains

OF CALAMITIES

REQUIEM

in the spring of 1970 two died as infants—
a requiem for control
brothers whose tiny hairs were woven into
a ring the likes of which were once set
upon the waves of the sea—two cosmically
pessimistic arias lifting the meaning of
chance (of grief) up—up towards myth
the spring of 1970 was of the same
maelstrom or arc the same sense of vertigo
this republic of ashes spat out or spat
upon fed on like played out horses
eye drawn to calamities with no promise
of recurrence or spot on a map famous
for its healing waters no safe place to draw
honey from the rock just the most sublime
forms of harmonious violence—
a hundred or thousand kinds of sadism
meant to draw the mouth to its master in a
fit of parasitic rage—an imaginary return to
the wound naturalized into an origin story of
innocence—a childlike remembrance at
the heart of the commonweal—a sucking
on the past for its proximity to
empty time when no one thought yet
to eat fire or defile the memory of a dead
language when no one thought yet of
the war metaphor not the forever war
but its prelude and coda separated by an
affectionate hand or hard kiss on the wound
seduced by the promise of sweetness and
its illusion of future importance—never
to venture across the street or ride a bus
alone into the valley of common recklessness

into the whole panoply of catastrophic
decisions and folds of prickly relations
expelled past the border sketched with a
fingernail around the surface of expectation
the horizon of understanding pushed
beyond the outermost contour
lifting civil war ballads from the thicket of
lost time and embedding them in snow
where no snow had ever landed
listening through the cold crack in the cement
wall where their portraits once hung—
listening for the hum or whistle of
disaster come calling down across the sky
we have written requiems for much less
elegies to flowers and bushes of flowers
with less blood on the leaves—
the body has been loaded upon again
and again and it only sucks further and
further into the mud like the lamb or lotus
given as a gift on the final day of reclamation
only to return upon the earth in the form
of a magpie milky from eating the flower
of decay—the body is a piano now rising
out of the sand and grass played poorly
by the wind but its sound or noise is that
of our nature scorning itself—the body
rings and groans played now with hammers
and tongs no mystic chords of memory or
sympathetic vibrations—the body unfurls like
after a long fire—an arm and then a hand a
finger and then a flake of skin or hair spoliated
by the melancholy progress of the wind

POEM WITH DRAWERS

in the backyard I found a nest (nothing special I
know) but it was in a vestigial light fixture from
when the house was built however many years ago
superfluities is the word John Winthrop used to describe
material possessions *abridge* he used to mean shave
away or cut like hair I tell people Ivanka Trump
named her child Arabella I don't know what I
expect them to get out of this I guess it was a canny
move on her part a speckled greenish egg among a
small ocean of eyelash-thin detritus: horsehair
scrap-paper dead grass I showed my wife a picture
when she came home and she said you're definitely
stoned she could tell by the music I was listening to—
Billy the Kid in one room and Captain Beefheart on in
the kitchen later that night I told her I was on the
Raymond Carver diet which she knew to mean all
weed and no booze—it's how I imagine he got straight
we are listening to the sound of helicopters overhead
a dog barks the conversation turns untellable and then
to photographic surveillance and the way in which men
assert their control over nature too often by deceitful
means never quite self-aware enough to cultivate an
elision or gap in our knowledge of either animals or
things—I dream of (daydream; long for) ancient or
oneiric times where I might have a little silhouette of
misunderstanding that I carry with me no photographic
or video evidence—only memory like a poem with
drawers but I can't help thinking that if we don't keep
touching these memories they'll fall off like fingernails
or a crow's bill or else throw themselves into the ocean
as William Bradford's wife Dorothy did when she laid
eyes on what would one day become America

ONLY ENDURANCE

me reading on the patio like the mime who
can only talk with a finger in his mouth naked
painting himself no more peregrinations in a
year full of them either drunk or sleep deprived
this is my philosophy of walking off the earth
(as I have seen in some temperance propaganda)
no hospital or gospels—only endurance

CRANIA AMERICANA

pray to nothing or maybe to the
video where the prime minister tells the
world that Franco's finally dead where do
we go after fascism an american Golgotha
awaits I wish I had hung art on these
walls framed magazine clippings
self-drawn portraits tesserae made from
cut up money—anything to absorb
the light and especially my attention I have
begun wearing only threadbare clothing
unbecoming as it is I can't bring myself
to buy to shed to procure only to fabricate
but I can't fabricate so I'll wrap myself
in a sheet dump myself down the
drain or onto a pyre enflamed by the idea
that we're still alive after what we've done
I could have invented a new language or
at least engaged in some kind of
cryptography but I'm no collagist or
puzzle-maker the whole world is
laughing at us in other words we have
the world's most slappable faces and I
think they could have laughed at us sooner—
for Andy Warhol maybe or for drinking
whisky with breakfast into the 1830s but
I wish you could have been there with
me when I painted the Pietà when I painted
the hammer that smashed the Pietà when I
painted Thomas Stearns Eliot (supposedly)
falling on his knees before the Pietà when
I painted the decline and fall of the
American empire as seen from a rest stop

on the 10 somewhere between Indio and
the Palo Verde Nuclear Generating Station
ca. 2020 or 2021 AD

BLACK SEA NIGHT

sleep is necessary or else we die from disunion or un-
repair it is 2:16 on the west coast I am unable to respond
I am trying to listen through what sounds like teeth-gritting
violin or viola music a sustained note hanging in the
air like the smell of a strange man the house is small but
paceable sloping west toward the capital of forgetting
every gesture down to utterance is a working toward
every error compounded by what are effectively homonyms
sympathetic cognates misapprehensions enigmas
modifications mortifications chord breaks fever lifts like
a hallucination or digression the mother reminds the
son that sleep is necessary or else we die deprived of
the waters or wellsprings that emerge from dreams it is 4:
56 and I have to turn the heater on a mist is rising
from the ground a punctured hose delivering its payload
to the universe a phrase works its way into the atmosphere:
suicide redeems the body I know it not to be true it is a
trick of the mind reminiscent of traducing the messiah in
order to be damned not out loud but in the depths of the
unconscious from where the holy father listens I listen
to the thrum in my brain listen for the sound of damning
also known as thunder sleep is necessary or else the body
goes rambling questing after similar sustenance three men
are smoking—articulated figures made of leather or
wood rudimentary in style and ascent emerging like wrack
from the world's oldest forest from beneath the sea from
before fish or cephalopods developed their gills I have
been damned and not damned—for traducing the messiah
for rambling and depriving for sleeping through long fits
for eating paper and spying like a wicked messenger from
behind stained glass the house is small but I roam from
window to window like an octopus centripetal in its

devouring it is 5:17 and the air is still…sun will be setting
like streaks of grease across the lens a negative landscape
celestial or otherwise appears exiled anonymous gracious in
its arduous silence

OF CALAMITIES

she implores me to stop reading about the old city—

ghosts and fractions of ghosts spread across the

cornea like surface hoar all slowly changing…

deceived by time or the idea of time I take the worst

of it or smallest flake and believe it—make it into

an origin story or moment of clarity carefully poised

between two theories of violence

PERISCOPE

there is a spider plant that only sort of half grows
I notice it as I gaze at the woman across the street
putting one of her children in the car I am drinking
water and smoking a very long cigarette like in a dream

it is irrational to be doing something like this the
father comes out not the child's father but the woman's
father or the father's father the so-called grandfather
now I am holding a piece of measuring tape fifty-nine (or

sixty) inches of it—it is symbolic in that it is whispering
in my ear reminding me that I have grown unhealthy
over the intervening years the father appears in his
overly ripe t-shirt and I wonder if they watch me like

this when I'm throwing out the beer bottles or pruning
the lemon tree sometimes I am watering and he is watering
but we don't acknowledge each other this is (I think) what
the sociologists call *gesellschaft*—no face-to-face interactions

or communitarian fealty family and neighborhood ties
sundered by modern tastes I think for a long while about
sex a realm of the mind better left unexplored a closet
stuffed or surfeited with shame and compulsion all I can

see are ties each one braided slightly different than the next
and shoes—some matte and some glinting like the moon
as seen through a periscope all held together with silver staples
I want to eat these things as a goat eats the mountainside

SONGS OF EXTREME SILENCE

I do not know what to expect from the earth
you may be trying to kill me how vague is death—
death by extreme silence death by hanging death by
border-war death by proxy put to death in absentia
we are no longer young we are waning our blood
should not pass uncelebrated our bodies should not
pass uncelebrated they say to have little ones little
private monsters who will grow to honor you
with their acts and deeds they say to mix water
and air to inaugurate the little beasts but in this
extreme heat (Siberia is no longer frozen) I do
not know what to expect from the oceans or the
forests I have taken my medicine—self-medicine
and regular and I have no idea what to expect
from my body and my body's future sometimes I
think my body is a canker on my life and then I
think my life is a canker on my body I can't get
straight who is doing the killing but the rivers are
growing with fish like children who grow strong—
strong like Orestes who killed his mother who will
put the coin under our tongues so that we can pay
the ferryman his wages I have been on a ferry
precisely once it was like a floating parking lot
dragging across the water and leaking french fry oil
they say the earth emerged from Chaos's womb
from Cronus' flint sickle from the blood of Uranus
estranged from his member the island was once a
mountain the bird was once a dinosaur the mirror
was once sand the tire was once a tree it is beginning
to look like there will be no one to avenge us like
Clytemnestra was by the Erinnyes who purified land
and sea with pig's blood and running water no one

to prosecute our murderers the watchful eye of
Athene has closed and the law once in the hands of
nature has been truly unloosed—God help us

THE NEW NEW TESTAMENT

I know it's a bit of a put-on
but who couldn't use a makeshift altar
a place to just *be*
you don't have to commune or even
come inside but maybe let the air
just blow across your shins
I'm not trying to summon angels
or even exactitude but the
world does end and we shouldn't go
about it casually and while we're not
going about it casually it is within
the realm of possibility to think not
only about solace but also grace—a
funny word to me now in my mouth
its legs ground to marble on an emery
wheel why not take it from door to
door or cave to cave take it even to
he who has a sign that says praying is
the best way to meet god—trespassing
is the fastest and has a printed hand
with a gun in it even he deserves to hear
about the long winter with no wheat or
the snowy road where you laid down
refusing to slaughter and eat the deer
why not sow the seeds of peace in
the ears of our detractors I may not be
the right messenger—a distillation of
everything wrong with the world but
there are ways to compromise with
whatever it means to be the devil at this
late date…the hill is laden with death
moths blot out the sun almost any

latecomer to the revolution could
tell you what happens next—paradise
extinguished not for the rest of time but
for what will feel like it we are worse
than fodder for the war we are worse
than lice we are like the butt end of a
joke or a grain of dust or dirt meant
to feed the engine of forgiveness forever
even as it hates your and my bones

WHAT GOES ON

we worry that someone will come to the door while
we're on our hands and knees *in extremis* entangled
having just discussed the way in which old Overholt
looks like G. Washington if he had lived to see A.
Jackson's old age we are making the sounds that

mourning doves make when they fly into power lines
not loud but engaged in a web of two or three things at
once no one comes to the door or peers through the
macramé to watch the two of us ropelike and enmeshed
on the couch no one struggles to imagine what we're

doing everyone is deep into their own primitive
experiments like Baudelaire who marked the difference
between sunlight and the darkness that lies beyond the
windowpane inviting us to look into each other's abyss—
the interior deep inside the imagination of disaster beyond

the dialectic of moral hygiene and electroconvulsive
therapy we close our eyes and imagine what lies beyond
the reaper's reach beyond religion or doubt beyond
sleep deprivation and underwater music and when
we finish fucking we sleep like the wind inside a cave

FROM THE MELTING PERMAFROST

this may be a final transmission or
second-to-last gasp maybe a cry for help an
accounting of everything I've seen up until
yesterday there is a lot to process right now
some things are too frightening to comprehend
like a wormhole into the past
have you ever been to Wilmington to Nauvoo
or Torrington to Alton where the last printing
press was shot into the earth's sky like a satellite
it is part of the trash nebula now there is
nothing romantic about finding water on the moon
but it may one day queer our grip on reality
Mike Davis critiqued Brecht for having never
set foot in a Wilmington bar and yet
here we are naturalizing the specter of a melancholy
wounding the seminal slaughter of ideals
thought good enough to colonize all aspects of
our institutional memory right down to the number
of bubbles in a bar of soap there will be calls for
blood and vengeance calls to reverse being
stabbed in the back—men out here from the
panhandle using semaphores and tongue-talkers
to engineer our demise my grandfather was a
ham radio enthusiast and my other grandfather
was a horse-breaker is there no room for me
now on this eerie plane of existence
the end will be cold and nomadic...the cultists
call down (from the afterlife) to say that
sleep is better than the talking cure
if we could behave like ghosts I'd take the beanpot
back into the field to collect pine nuts again
vanishing into the purple hands of my mother's

mother neither wading nor not wading into the
notion of an emerging insect world

TWO NOTES ON A PIANO

preserved undiluted light now barely-touched

reminiscent of dust floating fuguelike up and up

and now down-fingered apace declining in repose

two notes on a piano bracketed by forgetting

degrading over a length of tape or sinuous rope

stitched together…two notes only an oath

ACKNOWLEDGMENTS

Poems in *A Plea for Secular Gods* previously appeared in *Menacing Hedge*, *Grey Sparrow*, *Posit*, *Hinchas de Poesia*, *Inverted Syntax*, *The Shore*, *Oxidant|Engine*, *UCity Review*, *The Broadkill Review*, *New World Writing*, *Inflectionist Review*, *Josephine Quarterly*, *Watershed Review*, *Rhino Poetry*, *Pioneertown*, *Revolution John*, *A Hole in the Head Review*, *Blood Orange Review*, and *Kitchen Table Quarterly*.

BRYAN D. PRICE's work has appeared in *Diagram*, *Posit*, *Ucity Review*, *Rhino Poetry*, *Summerset Review*, and elsewhere. He has a PhD in History and may one day write the definitive history of nostalgia, which may perhaps come to be in the form of a poem. He lives in San Diego, with his wife, Claire, a dog (who shall remain nameless), and a cat named for Pina Bausch.

WHAT BOOKS PRESS

AN IMPRINT OF

THE GLASS TABLE

COLLECTIVE

LOS ANGELES

All WHAT BOOKS feature cover art by Los Angeles painter, printmaker, muralist, and theater and performance artist GRONK. A founding member of ASCO, Gronk collaborates with the LA and Santa Fe Operas and the Kronos Quartet. His work is found in the Corcoran, Smithsonian, LACMA, and Riverside Art Museum's Cheech Marin collection.

As a small, independent press, we urge our readers to support independent booksellers. This is easily done on our website by purchasing our books from Bookshop.org.

WHATBOOKSPRESS.COM

2023

God in Her Ruffled Dress
LISA B (LISA BERNSTEIN)
POEMS

Figures of Wood
MARÍA PÉREZ-TALAVERA
TRANSLATED BY PAUL FILEV
NOVEL

A Plea for Secular Gods: Elegies
BRYAN D. PRICE
POEMS

Nightfall Marginalia
SARAH MACLAY
POEMS

Romance World
TAMAR PERLA CANTWELL
STORIES

2022

No One Dies in Palmyra Ohio
HENRY ELIZABETH CHRISTOPHER
NOVEL

Us Clumsy Gods
ASH GOOD
POEMS

Skeletal Lights From Afar
FORREST ROTH
FLASH FICTION/PROSE POEMS

That Blue Trickster Time
AMY UYEMATSU
POEMS

2021

Pyre
MAUREEN ALSOP
POEMS

What Falls Away Is Always
KATHARINE HAAKE &
GAIL WRONSKY, EDITORS
ESSAYS

The Eight Mile
Suspended Carnival
REBECCA KUDER
NOVEL

Game
M.L. WILLIAMS
POEMS

2020

No, Don't
ELENA KARINA BYRNE
POEMS

One Strange Country
STELLA HAYES
POEMS

Remembering Dismembrance:
A Critical Compendium
DANIEL TAKESHI KRAUSE
NOVEL

Keeping Tahoe Blue
ANDREW TONKAVICH
STORIES

2019

Time Crunch
CATHY COLMAN
POEMS

Whole Night Through
L.I. HENLEY
POEMS

Echo Under Story
KATHERINE SILVER
NOVEL

Decoding Sparrows
MARIANO ZARO
POEMS

WHAT
BOOKS
PRESS

LOS ANGELES